Great White Sharks

By: Beth Costanzo

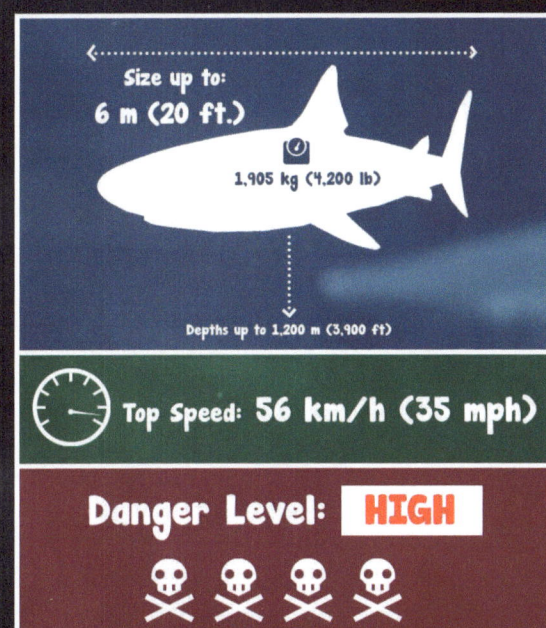

Size up to: 6 m (20 ft.)
1,905 kg (4,200 lb)
Depths up to 1,200 m (3,900 ft)

Top Speed: 56 km/h (35 mph)

Danger Level: **HIGH**
☠ ☠ ☠ ☠

☠ Great whites can detect a drop of blood in the water from 3 miles away.

Great White Shark

Great white sharks, like many other sharks, have rows of serrated teeth behind the main ones. The first two rows of the teeth are used for grabbing and cutting the animals they eat, while the other teeth in the last rows replace the front teeth when they are broken, worn down, or when they fall out. The teeth have the shape of a triangle with jags on the edges. Great white sharks eat fish and other animals, for example seals and sea lions.

The great white shark has no natural predators other than the Orca. Some orcas have discovered they can paralyse the shark by flipping it upside-down. Then they hold the shark still with their mouth, and that suffocates it (sharks get oxygen by moving through the water). That aside, they are apex predators of marine mammals.

www.adventuresofscubajack.com

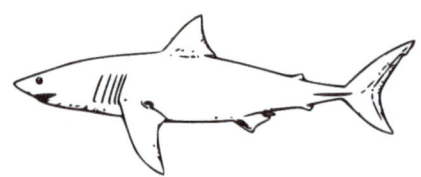

The **Great White Shark** is the world's largest known predatory fish, meaning it hunts for its food. It is powerful and aggressive. It is at the top of the ocean's food chain. Orca Whales or other Great White Sharks themselves are the only predator of a Great White Shark.

www.adventuresofscubajack.com

Sharks count on the element of surprise as they hunt. When they see a seal at the water, sharks will often position themselves underneath the seal. Using their tails as propellers, they swim upward at a fast sprint, burst out of the water in a leap called a *breach*, and fall back into the water with the seal in their mouth.

www.adventuresofscubajack.com

At birth a **baby** *Great White Shark* is about *five feet* long. When a *Great White Shark* is born, along with up to twelve siblings, it immediately swims away from its mother. It lives on its own immediately. A mother may see her newborn sharks as prey.

www.adventuresofscubajack.com

Most people fear the *Great White Shark* and consider it a *man-eater*, but shark attacks usually happen because sharks confuse humans with seals. A Great White gives a *"test-bite,"* but it is unlikely that it keeps eating once it finds unusual food.

www.adventuresofscubajack.com

Great White Sharks live and hunt on the coast of every continent in the world except Antarctica. They prefer to live in cooler waters with temps ranging from *54-75 degrees.*

commons.wikimedia.org

www.adventuresofscubajack.com

Great White Sharks are decreasing in numbers and are rare due to years of being hunted by man for fins and teeth. They are also seen as a trophy for sport fishing. Great Whites are often caught in nets or entangled in mesh that protects the beach.

www.adventuresofscubajack.com

TEN FUN FACTS ABOUT GREAT WHITE SHARKS

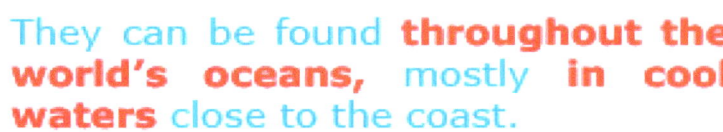

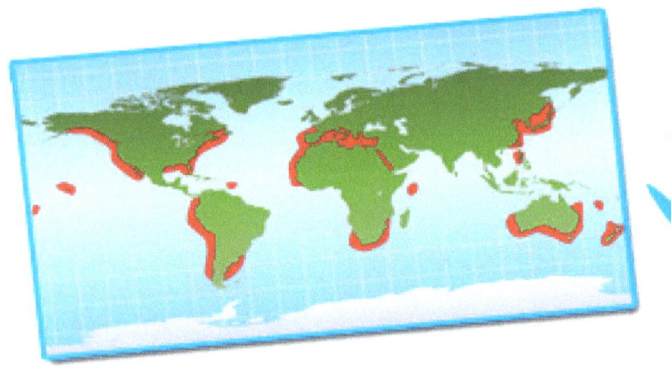

1 They can be found **throughout the world's oceans,** mostly **in cool waters** close to the coast.

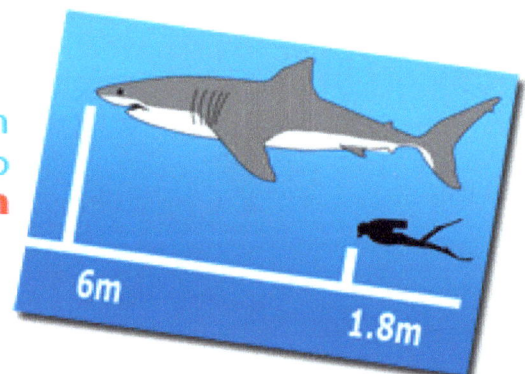

2 They are the **largest predatory** fish on our planet. On average, they grow to around **4.6m long,** but sometimes **6m** – that's half the length of a bus!

3 Great white sharks are **grey with a white underbelly.** They have a streamlined shape and powerful tails that propel them through the water at over **60km per hour!**

4 Their mouth is equipped with a set of **300 sharp, triangular teeth** arranged in up to **seven rows.** Yikes!

5 They are not fearsome man-eaters. **Phew!** There are around **5-10 attacks a year,** but researchers believe that the sharks are instead taking a **"sample bite"** out of curiosity, before swimming off.

www.adventuresofscubajack.com

TEN FUN FACTS ABOUT GREAT WHITE SHARKS

6 **Young** white sharks feed on small prey, such as **fish and rays**. But when they're **older and bigger**, they generally feast on sea mammals such as **sea lions, seals and small whales**.

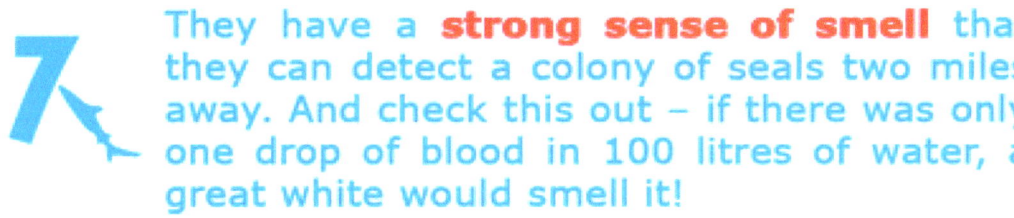

7 They have a **strong sense of smell** that they can detect a colony of seals two miles away. And check this out – if there was only one drop of blood in 100 litres of water, a great white would smell it!

8 They like to **take their prey by surprise**. They usually position themselves underneath their unsuspecting victims before swimming up and…chomp! They often burst out of the water in a leap (called a breach) before falling back in with their meal in their mouths.

9 When a great white gives **birth**, she usually has **two to ten youngsters, called "pups"**. But she shows no care for her offspring – in fact, she may even try to eat them! Taking care of themselves, the newborn pups will immediately swim off into the ocean.

10 They are at **the top of the food chain** and aren't likely to be killed by other sea creatures. Sadly, however, they are under serious threat by human activity. Illegal hunting of these beautiful beasts, and overfishing, have meant that today they are an **endangered species**.

www.adventuresofscubajack.com

More Great White Shark Fun Facts

- Great White Sharks can smell a single drop of blood up to one-third of a mile away.

- Great White Sharks are carnivores and prey on other sea creatures like seals, sea birds, dolphins, Tuna Fish and some species of whales.

- It has 300 teeth, yet does not chew its food.

- The Great White has an average life span of 25 years.

- Adult females grow larger than males, which are usually 2 meters smaller.

- They have three major fins: Caudal fin, Pectoral fin and Dorsal fin.

- Great White Sharks don't chew their food. They rip off chunks of meat and swallow them whole.

- They are warm-blooded and regulate their own body temperature.

- The Great White has nostrils on the underside of its snout.

- Great Whites have two small openings behind and above their eyes that work as outer ears.

- A baby Great White is called a pup.

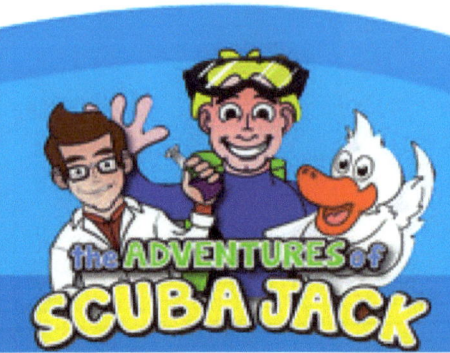

TEST YOUR SMARTS ON GREAT WHITE SHARKS

TRUE OR FALSE?

☐ Great white Sharks have been measured at 2m long

☐ Great white sharks are red with a white underbelly

☐ Great white sharks have 30 sharp, triangular teeth arranged in up to seven rows.

www.adventuresofscubajack.com

HAVE FUN WITH GREAT WHITE SHARKS

COLOR YOUR GREAT WHITE SHARK

www.adventuresofscubajack.com

HAVE FUN WITH GREAT WHITE SHARKS

TRACE THE WORDS BELOW

GREAT WHITE SHARK

GREAT WHITE SHARK

GREAT WHITE SHARK

great white shark

great white shark

great white shark

www.adventuresofscubajack.com

HAVE FUN WITH GREAT WHITE SHARKS

WHITE SHARKY IS SO HUNGRY CAN YOU HELP HIM GET ITS MEAL !!

www.adventuresofscubajack.com

HAVE FUN WITH GREAT WHITE SHARKS

WHITE SHARKS WORD SEARCH

```
P X B R D G L F H L W X
M U L R W F V L O Y H K
A A V C A X J E V F I N
M P K N E C J V E G T U
M H P Q P Y G B R S E J
A K Y N V P L K F E S K
L V R Z R Y T D I A H O
S D J V J P U P S L A C
W H A L E S F X H I R E
S E A L E R E E I O K A
F O O D C H A I N N T N
O S Y O X E W Y G B S S
```

WHITE SHARK SEA LION SEAL
OCEANS WHALES MAMMALS PUPS
FOOD CHAIN OVERFISHING FIN

www.adventuresofscubajack.com

HAVE FUN WITH GREAT WHITE SHARKS

GREAT WHITE SHARKS DOT TO DOT

www.adventuresofscubajack.com

HAVE FUN WITH GREAT WHITE SHARKS

MAKE YOUR WHITE SHARKY WITH SCISSORS

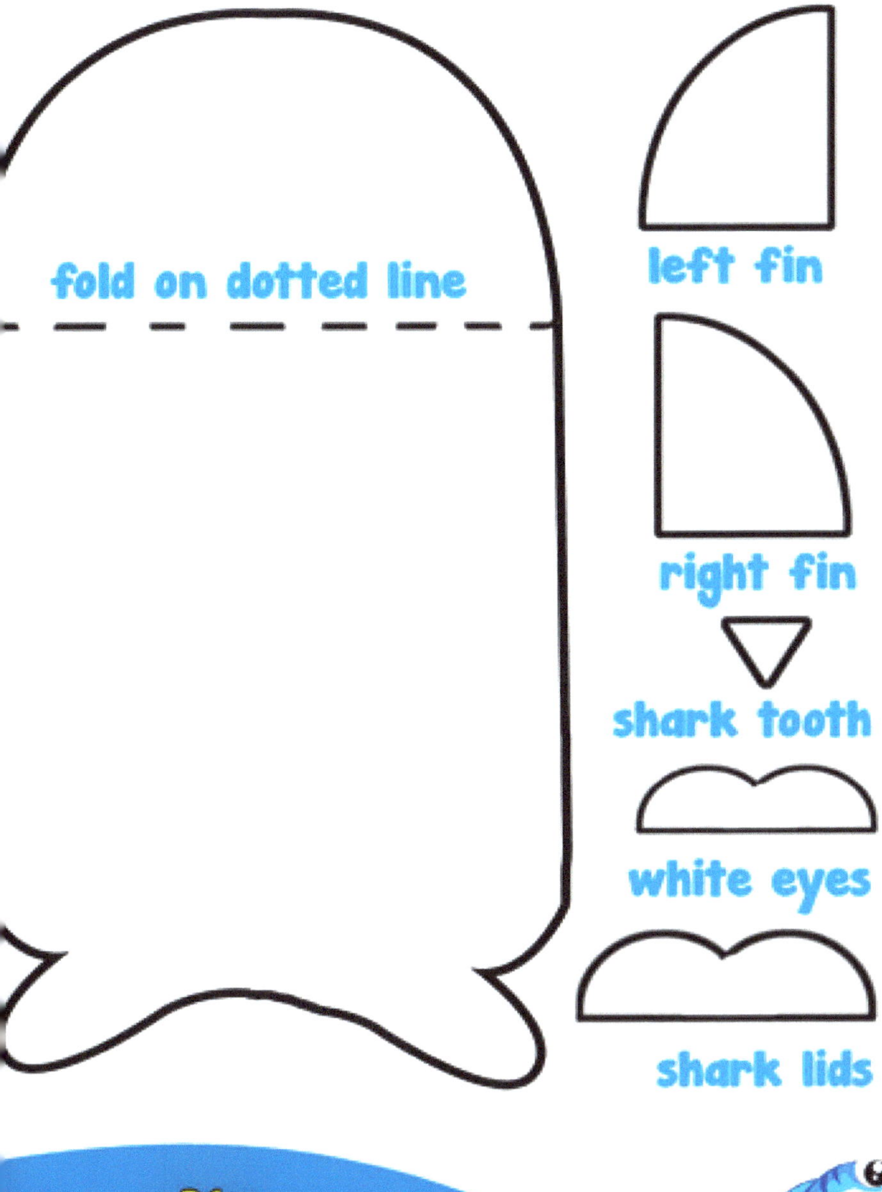

fold on dotted line

left fin

right fin

shark tooth

white eyes

shark lids

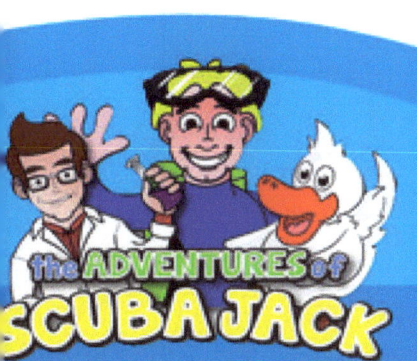

www.adventuresofscubajack.com

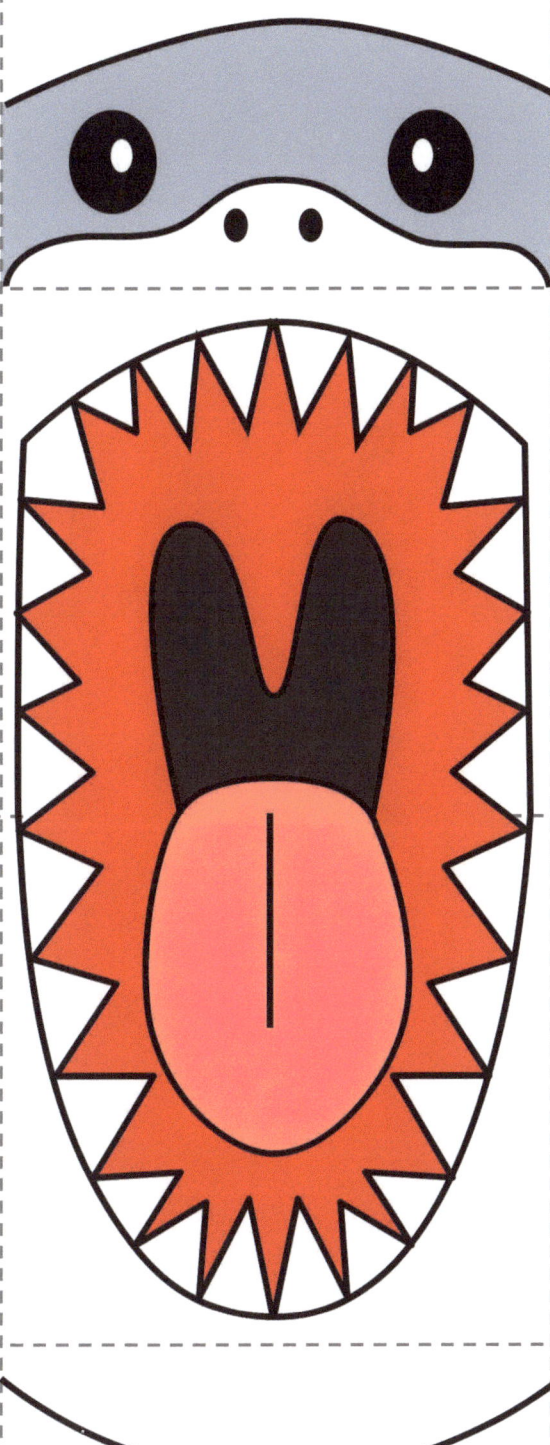

GLUE

www.adventuresofscubajack.com

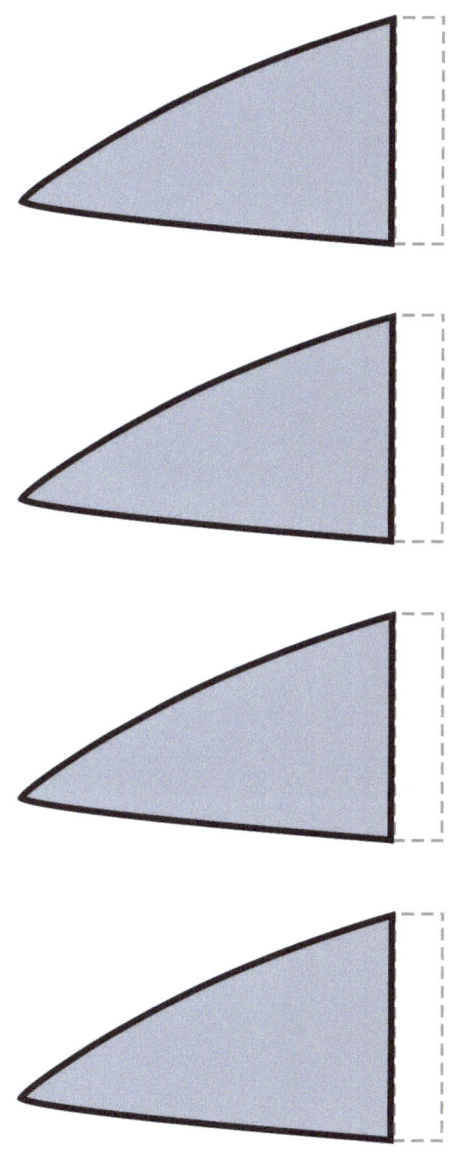
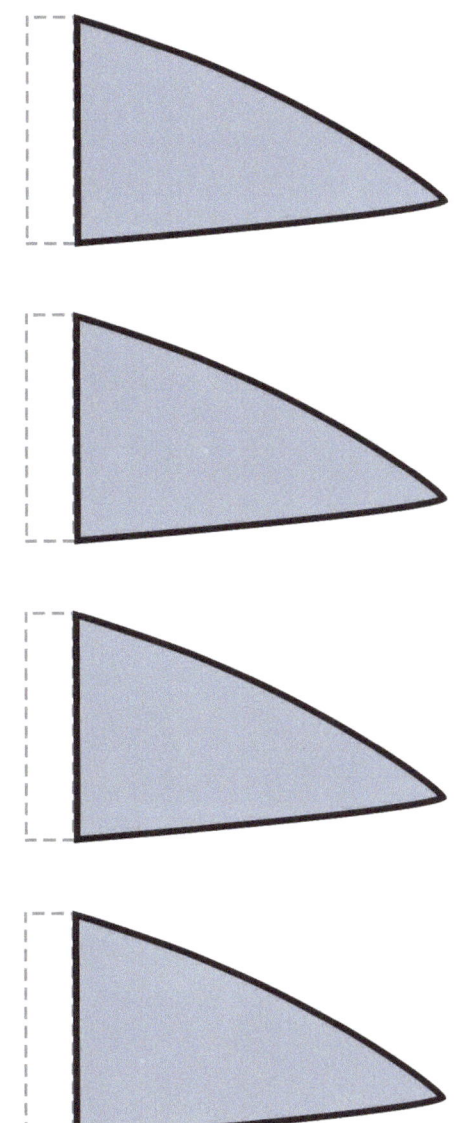

www.adventuresofscubajack.com

Video & Quiz are in our website:

www.adventuresofscubajack.com

Under «**Read To Me**» section

www.ingramcontent.com/pod-product-compliance
Lightning Source LLC
Chambersburg PA
CBHW041439010526
44118CB00002B/121